# I SPY SPORTS!

© 2023 Webber Books

All rights reserved. This book or any portion thereof may not be reproduced or used in any manner whatsoever without the express written permission of the publisher except for the use of brief quotations in a book review.

# Welcome to I SPY SPORTS!

# GOOD LUCK!

# I SPY with my little eye, something beginning with...

# M
### is for
# MEDAL!

# I SPY with my little eye, something beginning with...

# B
### is for
# BASKETBALL!

# I SPY with my little eye, something beginning with...

# I SPY with my little eye, something beginning with...

P is for PADDLES!

# I SPY with my little eye, something beginning with...

# I SPY with my little eye, something beginning with...

# F is for FLAG!

# I SPY with my little eye, something beginning with...

i is for ICE SKATER!

# I SPY with my little eye, something beginning with...

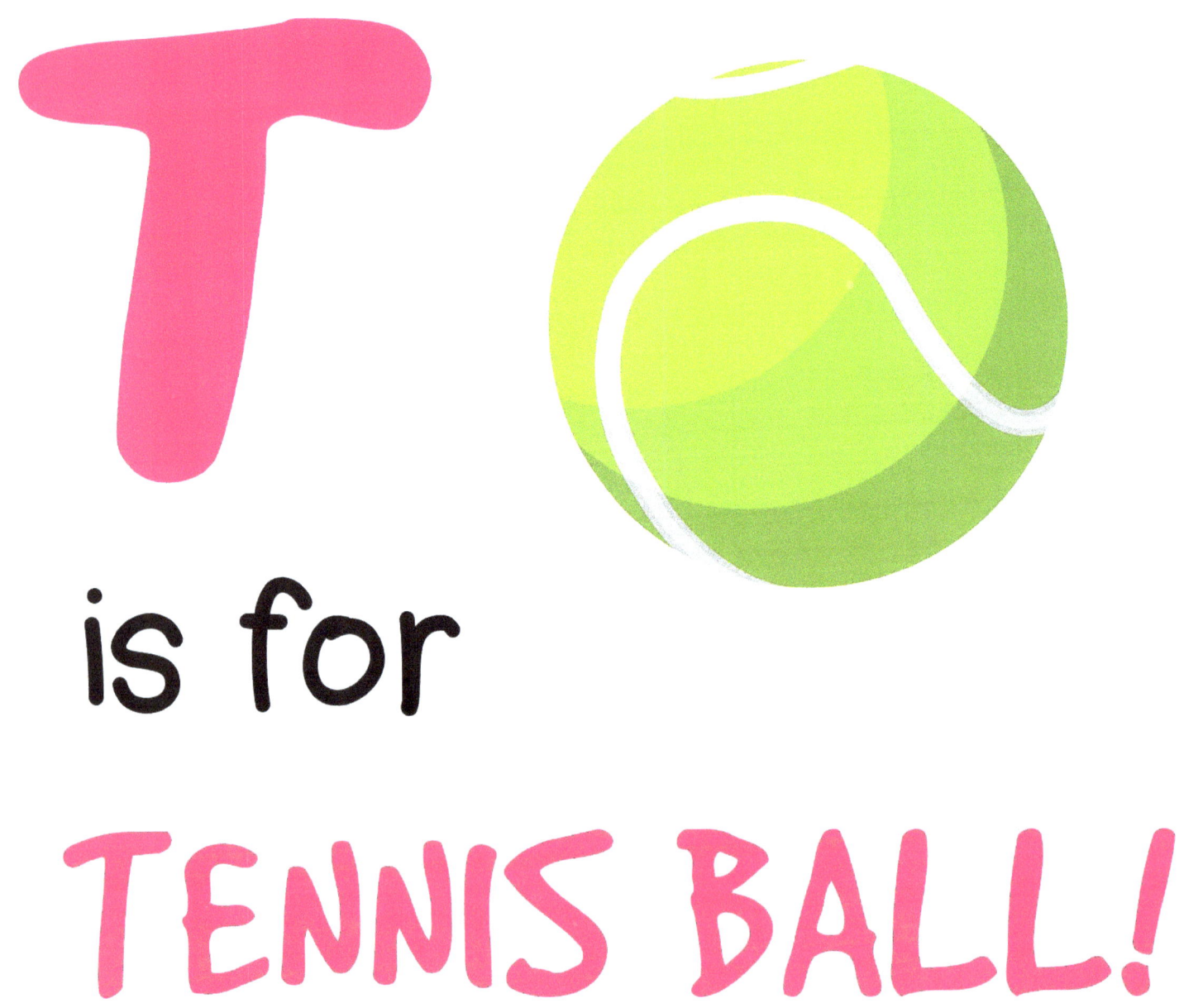

# I SPY with my little eye, something beginning with... K

# I SPY with my little eye, something beginning with...

J is for JIGSAW!

# I SPY with my little eye, something beginning with...

# I SPY with my little eye, something beginning with... C

# I SPY with my little eye, something beginning with...

Y is for Yo-Yo!

# I SPY with my little eye, something beginning with...

D is for DARTBoARD!

# I SPY with my little eye, something beginning with...

# I SPY with my little eye, something beginning with...

# G

### is for

# GLOVES!

# THE END!

www.ingramcontent.com/pod-product-compliance
Lightning Source LLC
Chambersburg PA
CBHW051321110526
44590CB00031B/4430